CHEVY
55-56-57

Mike Mueller

Motorbooks International
Publishers & Wholesalers®

First published in 1993 by Motorbooks International Publishers & Wholesalers, PO Box 2, 729 Prospect Avenue, Osceola, WI 54020 USA

Motorbooks International books are also available at discounts in bulk quantity for industrial or sales-promotional use. For details write to Special Sales Manager at the Publisher's address

Printed and bound in Hong Kong

Library of Congress Cataloging-in-Publication Data

Mueller, Mike.
    Chevy 55-56-57 / Mike Mueller.
        p.   cm. — (Enthusiast color series)
    Includes index
    ISBN 0-87938-816-1
    1. Chevrolet automobile—History. I. Title. II. Title: Chevy fifty-five, fifty-six, fifty-seven. III. Series.
TL215.C48M84   1993
629.222'2'0973—dc20   93-17024

On the front cover: A trio of Chevrolet's best-loved cars pose in the Florida sunshine. Chevy's look struck a chord with the American motoring public in 1955 and was carefully refined over the next two years.

On the frontispiece: Perhaps the best known fin of the fifties. Clever design flourishes like this hidden fuel filler were a hallmark of fifties design.

On the title page: Admit it. You wanted to see these three again. Twin spotlights, among other accessories, grace each of these cars.

On the back cover: The classic Nomad. Although not as popular as the 1957 coupe, sedan, or convertible versions when new, Nomads are highly sought-after collectibles today.

Contents

Simply Classic

Save for perhaps Corvettes and Ford's two-seat Thunderbirds, no American automobiles are as coveted, loved, and worshipped as 1955–1957 Chevrolets. Find someone who doesn't recognize a '57 Chevy and you have a story. Less well-known among casual observers, the legendary "Hot One" of 1955—progenitor of the classic Chevy triumvirate—is widely revered among enthusiasts for its historical significance, as well as its ever-present potential as a wild street machine. Situated between, the '56 Chevy tends to get lost in the shadows, but it is as much a classic as its more popular cousins.

Explaining the classic Chevy phenomenon isn't easily done. During the same time span Fords were equally popular, insofar as sales figures were concerned. To this day, many Ford fanatics shake their heads wondering why their favorite cars are seemingly slighted by history, overshadowed by the hated Tri-Chevys. But facts can't be denied, and the plain truth was that in 1955 Chevrolet got the all-important jump in the rapidly forming youth market.

Although Ford was first in the low-priced field with an overhead-valve V-8 in 1954, Chevy's new ohv V-8 introduced the following year was superior—an innovative, short-stroke powerplant with loads of performance potential. They didn't call the '55 Chevy the "Hot One" for nothing. Ford's "Y-block" V-8 was heavy, a bit outdated, and didn't respond well to performance modifications. In contrast, Chevrolet impressed everyone with its fresh brand of affordable get-up-and-go. A triple-digit top end had never been this cheap, nor had loads of style and heavy doses of modern engineering. Simply put, once the '55 Chevy came along, Detroit was never the same again.

Adding more powerful performance

options in 1956 only helped solidify Chevrolet's newfound popularity among young, excitable buyers, and it wasn't long before Chevy's muscular small-block V-8 had become the hot rodder's choice. Creating a truly classic design in 1957 essentially assured continued popularity with generations to follow.

Today, classic Chevrolet club members number in the hundreds of thousands and support from the restoration industry is virtually unmatched. As a curbside wag might point out, with so many parts available through the reproduction market, it may well be possible to see more '55-57 Chevys on the road today than were originally built. Even if that were true, few would probably care—save for a Ford follower or two.

Acknowledgments

As usual, we can't even consider beginning this book until hearty thanks are offered to all the people who graciously allowed their beautiful classic Chevys to be photographed for these pages. Their patience and cooperation was wholly appreciated. In order of appearance, they are:

Larry Young, Port Charlotte, Florida: '55 Bel Air convertible, '56 Bel Air hardtop, and '57 Bel Air convertible; Don Allen, Winter Haven, Florida: '55 Bel Air hardtop; Gene Jr., Sherri, and Christie DeBlasio, Plantation, Florida: '55 Nomad; Walter Cutlip, Longwood, Florida: '56 Bel Air convertible; Fred Gaugh, Polk City, Florida, Terry Sheafer and Jerome Cain, Lakeland, Florida: '56 Bel Air hardtop (with Corvette V8); Dave Johnson, Clearwater, Florida: '56 Nomad; Bruce and Linda Finley, Lakeland, Florida: '57 Bel Air convertible; Lloyd Brekke, Winter Haven, Florida: '57 Bel Air hardtop; Bill and Barbara Jacobsen, Silver Dollar Classic Cars, Odessa, Florida: '57 210 sedan; Rich Miller, Clearwater, Florida: '57 fuel-injected Bel Air convertible; Erol and Susan Tuzcu, Del Ray Beach, Florida: '57 Nomad.

Chapter 1

1955

The Hot One Hits Town

General Motors' Chevrolet division was no stranger to sales success by the time the all-new 1955 models appeared. Dependent upon how the numbers were juggled, Chevrolet had been Detroit's sales leader for nineteen consecutive years—at least according to admen in 1954 (Ford also claimed the title that year). As affordable, dependable, economical cars, Chevys couldn't be beat in the early fifties, though a strong push by Ford had matched Chevrolet virtually step-for-step in the low-priced field from 1953 on.

As the fifties progressed, however, it became apparent that Chevrolet's venerable "Stovebolt" image would not survive as a main selling point with prestige, power, and pizzazz growing in popularity. In the thoroughly modern postwar market, GM was consistently on the cutting edge each year with styling breakthroughs and engineering advancements. Even at the bottom of GM's pecking order, the low-priced Chevrolets wouldn't be left out. As early as December 1951, GM's engineering brain trust had determined it was time to turn Chevrolet around. Six months later, former Cadillac V-8 engineer Ed Cole took charge of Chevrolet's engineering crew. The rest, as they say, is history.

Opposite page
Attractive two-toning suited the '55 Chevy to a tee. This dazzling India Ivory/Gypsy Red combination was one of twenty-three two-tone combos offered in 1955, along with fourteen solid-color schemes. Beneath all that beauty dwelt a revamped chassis featuring a rigid frame, ball joint front suspension, a revised rear leaf spring arrangement, and large drum brakes. Superior inside and out, the '55 Chevy left *Motor Trend* flustered: "Should we talk about the car's acceleration, its brakes, its handling? Or discuss its interior, its styling, its ride?"

"Everything's new everywhere you look" claimed Chevrolet ads in praise of the totally redesigned, totally restyled "Motoramic" '55 Chevy. Equally attractive beneath its skin, the car was described by *Mechanix Illustrated*'s Tom McCahill as "the most glamorous looking and hottest performing Chevy to come down the pike." Chevy's first modern overhead-valve V-8 (the company's first V-8 had come and gone some thirty-five years before) inspired the legendary "Hot One" nickname.

Cole and company created Chevrolet's first modern overhead-valve V-8, transforming Chevys from the cars your grandpa drove into some of the hottest machines on 1955 roads. "We find it hard to believe it's a descendant of previous Chevrolets," stated *Motor Trend*. Cole's 265ci V-8, combined with a long list of mechanical refinements and fresh styling that startled almost every-

one, helped power the all-new '55 Chevy into the limelight not only as a low-priced leader, but also as a fine-performing, attractive automobile anyone would enjoy driving.

Suddenly buyers in the low-price field had a choice. "Chevrolet's stylists, engineers and sales personnel are out to give the public exactly what they want in 1955," explained a *Motor Life* report. In standard six-cylinder form, Chevys remained available as budget-minded, economical, everyday transportation. On the other hand, if a customer wanted more, more was available in spades. Styling was dreamy—a direct reflection of GM's Motorama dream-car designs—and

The Bel Air two-door sport coupe was one of the more popular Chevrolet models in 1955 with a production total of 185,562. Only the Bel Air four-door sedan (345,372) and two lower-priced 210 series models, the 210 four-door sedan (317,724) and two-door sedan (249,105), topped that total. List price for a V-8-equipped '55 Bel Air sport coupe was $2,166.

The venerable Blue Flame six-cylinder, offered in two forms dependent upon transmission choice, remained as standard power for the '55 Chevy. Backed by a three-speed manual transmission, the Blue Flame six was rated at 123hp. Output increased to 136hp with the optional Powerglide automatic. Both engines featured 7.5:1 compression and one-barrel carburetors.

Right
These attractive wheel covers were standard equipment for 1955's top-of-the-line Bel Air models. The lower-priced 150 and 210 models came standard with small center caps. Optional wheel trim rings and chrome wire wheel covers were also available.

top-line Bel Air hardtops and convertibles showed off the new look in classy fashion. Performance was excellent, thanks to 162hp from the base 265ci, or 180hp with the optional four-barrel carburetor and dual exhausts. To top it all off, Chevrolet even offered a sporty two-door station wagon, the Nomad, a design that first appeared on 1954's Motorama stage (based on a Corvette platform).

Compliments and praise for the '55 Chevy were almost endless, but Chevrolet advertisements summed it up best when they labeled the all-new offering the "Hot One."

V-8-powered '55 Chevrolets were easily identified from the rear by the small "V" emblems beneath each taillight. Choosing the 162hp, 265ci V-8 added about $100 to the bottom line. The chrome exhaust extension for this 162hp Turbo-Fire V-8 was a $3.25 dealer-installed accessory. The bumper's fender guards were also a dealer accessory, a front and rear set costing $39.

One of the principle objectives of the 1955 styling, and perhaps its most striking feature, is the car's look of mobility at all times. This is true from every aspect, and is especially evident in the front end design . . .

—*1955 Chevrolet Features*

The Ferrari-inspired "egg-crate" grille—reportedly included in Chevrolet's new design at Harley Earl's insistence—wasn't particularly popular among dealers as chrome and more chrome was "in" at the time. Optional pieces shown here include the front fender guards at each corner of the bumper (rear fender guards were also available) and an accompanying grille guard.

The '55 Bel Air's modern and reasonably plush interior featured various two-tone cloth upholstery combinations and a sporty, "twin cowl" dashboard layout that mimicked the design first used on the '53 Corvette. Running the width of the dash was a bright applique embossed with 987 mini "Bow-Ties," Chevrolet's ever-present logo.

The heart of the Hot One, the 265ci ohv V-8. Thanks to its short stroke and innovative ball-stud rocker arm assembly—a design borrowed from Pontiac that helped reduce reciprocating weight—the 265ci small-block could wind with the best of them without coming undone at high rpms. The 162hp maximum came at 4400rpm. Compression was a healthy 8:1. Compact, lightweight, and easy to manufacture, the 265ci V-8 represented, in *Motor Life's* words, "the last word in producing a complicated 8 cylinder engine at a price competitive with the most inexpensive powerplants in the industry."

Following pages
Chevrolet's 1955 convertible sales doubled 1954's figures, reaching 41,292 for the '55 Bel Air drop-top. List price for a V-8-equipped convertible was $2,305. The bright, twin exhaust extensions give away the presence of the optional 180hp 265ci four-barrel V-8. Additional added-cost items include fender skirts, wire wheel covers, twin spotlights, front fender gravel guards, sill moldings, and a typically fifties Continental kit.

17

Left
Undoubtedly more popular today than thirty-five years ago, Continental spare-tire carriers are now common sights on restored '55-57 Chevys. This eye-catching $120 option made more room in the trunk as the typical spare location was vacated.

Included on a long list of dress-up options for the '55 Chevy was this chrome wire wheel cover, complete with Chevrolet Bow-Tie logo in the center.

21

Spotlights, either single or in pairs, were
available over dealer counters or through various
aftermarket suppliers.

This rare centrally located dashboard compass was a $3.57 option in 1955.

Right
Another popular fifties option was this $2.90, dash-mounted, prismatic traffic light viewer which allowed the driver to conveniently see an overhead traffic light's color.

T he Motoramic Chevrolet is more than a new car. It's a completely new concept of low-cost motoring—without parallel in automotive history.
—*1955 Specifications Catalog for Chevrolet Salesmen*

The passenger half of the '55 Chevy's attractive, symmetrical "twin-cowl" dash layout incorporated a radio speaker and a clock the driver couldn't possibly read. Notice the many small Bow-Tie logos incorporated in the dashboard appliqué.

Right
Fitted with the optional $60 "Power Pak" consisting of a four-barrel carburetor and dual exhausts, the 265ci V-8 jumped to 180hp from its standard 162hp rating. According to *Road and Track* tests, a 180hp '55 sedan with a three-speed overdrive transmission and 4.11:1 gears could run 0–60mph in 9.7sec. Quarter-mile time was 17.4sec.

The luxurious sitting-room comfort, modern-living convenience, and tasteful beauty inside the Motoramic Chevrolet exceed the greatest expectations.

—1955 Specifications Catalog for Chevrolet Salesmen

Convertible 1955 Bel Airs featured more stylish seats with distinctive pleating and a different two-tone design than those used in closed cars. Notice the tissue dispenser below the radio and beneath the dash—one of many added-cost baubles on this nicely decked-out '55 drop-top.

Previous pages
When General Motors' styling mogul Harley Earl
saw designer Carl Renner's sketches for a sporty
station wagon roofline in 1953, he instructed his
men to translate the idea into reality as a

Corvette-based show car for GM's 1954
Motorama extravaganza. The result was the so-
called "Waldorf Nomad," a two-door Corvette
station wagon named for the site of its
introduction, New York's Waldorf Astoria

An exclusive tailgate design featuring seven chrome trim bars became a Nomad wagon trademark. This trim was also accompanied by gold "Nomad" script above the gate handle. Yet another carry-over from the Motorama show car was the roof's ribbed rear section. Nomads also lacked the typical beltline dip found just behind the doors on other '55 Chevrolet models.

Left

Save for the unique bodyside trim that began as headlight brows and extended back into the doors, a '55 Nomad featured standard Bel Air sheet metal and trim from the cowl forward. Remaining body components, however, were another story entirely. Most obvious was the two-door body and stylish roofline with sloping pillars. Glass area was extensive, adding to the sporty look. The roof and full wheel openings were direct carry-overs from 1954's Corvette Nomad Motorama show car.

Hotel. Enthusiastic response on the show circuit inspired Earl to ask for a regular-production '55 passenger car version of the Nomad. Priced at $2,571, Chevrolet's Nomad sport wagon attracted 8,530 buyers in 1955.

Air conditioning—an exceptionally rare convenience option due primarily to its extremely high price (upwards of $500)—was a feature worth bragging about in 1955, a task performed by a wing window decal on this Skyline Blue '55 Nomad.

Right
Among the many optional features on this fully loaded '55 Nomad are these three items: the $2.90 prismatic traffic light viewer (left), the $44.25 autronic eye automatic headlight dimmer, and twin spotlights.

Looking very much like a crowded, modern-day engine compartment, this Nomad's underhood spaces are packed to the rafters thanks to a complete array of optional equipment. Taking up the majority of room on the passenger's side is the air conditioning unit and compressor, while the driver's side is occupied by both power steering (mounted at the generator's rear) and power brakes.

Right
For 1955 only, Nomads featured exclusive interior treatments. Although the dashboard was typical '55 Bel Air equipment, upholstery and door panels incorporated a unique pleated and waffled vinyl design. Equally unique were chrome head-liner bows, which appeared in '56 and '57 as well. Notice the air conditioning outlet just below the dogleg doorpost on the passenger side.

Left
Unlike the Nomad models to follow in 1956 and '57, Chevrolet's first sporty, two-door wagon body involved more modifications than the simple addition of the airy top and sloping tailgate. Fully rounded rear wheel openings, copied from the non-running Motorama show car, were another original Nomad trademark.

Linoleum covered the Nomad's storage area, including the rear seatback which folded down to maximize cargo capacity. Spare-tire location was beneath a lift-up floor panel just inside the tailgate.

Chapter 2

1956

Turning Up The Heat

Chevrolet kicked off the 1956 model year in a shower of gravel and dust as famed Corvette engineer Zora Arkus-Duntov dashed up Colorado's Pikes Peak in a disguised '56 Bel Air sedan. His time to the top was two minutes less than any previous American stock sedan effort, an unofficial record performance that proved Chevrolet wasn't about to rest on its laurels. If people thought the '55 Chevy was hot, they hadn't seen nothing yet.

Ads for the new '56 Chevy claimed "the hot one's even hotter," and they weren't blowing smoke. Big news for 1956 involved the introduction of the "Super Turbo-Fire" V-8, based on the same 265ci small-block introduced in '55, but with twenty-five more horses than the previous year's top-rated "Power Pak" version. One bout behind the wheel of a 205hp '56 Chevy and *Mechanix Illustrated*'s Tom McCahill couldn't say enough. Calling the car the "best perfor-

mance buy in the world," he claimed it "would whiz by a Duesenberg like Halley's Comet [and] the vacuum as it went by would suck the stork off a Hispano-Suiza." *Road and Track* posted performance figures of 0–60mph in 9.0sec and 16.6sec at 108.7mph for the quarter-mile. Impressive, sure, but there was more.

In January 1956 Chevrolet announced it would be optionally installing the Corvette's newly introduced dual four-barrel V-8 in the regular passenger car line. Rated at 225hp, the optional Corvette powerplant had

Opposite page
Like Chevrolet's '55 models, the '56 Nomad used small "V" emblems below each taillight to signify the presence of the 265ci V-8. Other '56 V-8 models had one large "V" on the deck lid or tailgate. Base price for a '56 Nomad wagon was $2,707.

Left
If there were any complaints concerning the '55 Chevy it was the small "egg-crate" grille up front, a design quite contrary to American norms of the time. Beyond offending sensibilities, veteran road tester Floyd Clymer saw the grille as a maintenance problem. "Looks like you'll need a bottle brush to keep each square clean," he wrote. Clymer also pointed out that 15 percent of '55 Chevy customers polled wanted the grille changed. Designers did just that for '56, stretching the grille full width and enlarging the individual squares. Overall, the '56 Chevrolet took on a new, fresh look with relatively minor styling changes.

Although total sales dropped by more than 200,000 units, Chevrolet still managed to outsell arch-rival Ford by about a quarter-million models—in '55 Chevy's lead had only been 70,000 cars. After interviewing various Ford and Chevrolet dealers in 1956, *Fortune* magazine helped explain the situation, reporting that while Ford had come back in '56 with a nearly identical rendition of its '55 model, Chevy "made more of a change." This India Ivory/Nassau Blue Bel Air is one of 41,268 convertibles built for 1956. Base price was $2,443. Chrome-tipped dual exhaust is an owner-installed item.

McCahill returning for a second opinion. "Chevrolet has come up with a poor man's answer to a hot Ferrari," he wrote. "Here's an engine that can wind up tighter than the

E-string on an East Laplander's mandolin, well beyond 6000 rpm without blowing up like a pigeon egg in a shotgun barrel. Zero to 30 averages 3.2 seconds, 0-60 8.9 seconds,

and in 12 seconds you're doing 70. This is just about May, June and July faster than the Chevrolets of just two or three years ago."

In July, Jerry Unser ramrodded a 225hp '56 Chevy up Pikes Peak in an official time of 16min 8sec, 1min 16sec better than Arkus-Duntov's earlier run.

Clearly, the heat had been turned up, but a stronger V-8 wasn't the only news for 1956. Lightly revamped styling offered what some felt was an even fresher look, although the '56 Chevy was hard pressed to top the popularity of its forerunner. Up front, the small, unpopular egg-crate grille was replaced by a "more American" full-width unit, while new taillights in back weren't quite so plain as in '55. Overall, the '56 Chevy was a package that did its bloodline proud, even if many today overlook it in favor of the classic '55 and '57 renditions.

Little changed inside the '56 Chevy as far as the instrument panel was concerned, save for the dashboard appliqué design on which the mini Bow-Ties were exchanged for columns of rectangles. Different door panels and modified upholstery styles represented quick make-overs.

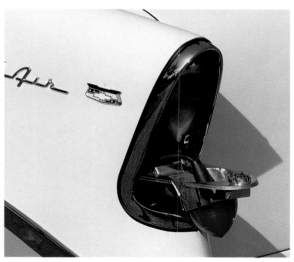

Demonstrating the design cleverness typical of many fifties cars, the '56 Chevrolet's fuel filler was moved from the driver's side rear quarter panel and hidden behind the driver's side taillight. Twisting a latch above the taillight released the hinged assembly and exposed the fuel tank filler neck.

Far left
Chevrolet's growing bag of added-cost baubles for 1956 included these $5.58 "fender birds." This optional front-fender top molding joined the full array of bumper guards, stone shields, and other decorative trim pieces.

As with interior treatments, standard '56 Bel Air full wheel covers carried over from 1955.

Left
In standard trim, the 265ci Turbo-Fire V-8 was rated differently dependent upon the transmission selected. As in '55, the rating was 162hp with a three-speed manual installed. Shown here is the 170hp version, which is mated to the optional Powerglide automatic. Both engine featured two-barrel carburetors and 8:1 compression.

O n straightaway runs and around closed circuits it takes power and control to stay out in front. And the Chevrolet V-8 has what it takes.
—*Motor Life, March 1956*

Following pages
In reference to the '56 Chevrolet, *Car Life* claimed that "people who like the car in 1955 will like it even more so this year, and for the same basic reasons." Tastefully revamped styling made the '56 models appear longer and less heavy. An attractive Bel Air four-door sport sedan was added to the 1956 model line and attracted 104,602 buyers. Production of '56 Bel Air sport coupes, like this Adobe Beige/Sierra Gold example, was 128,382.

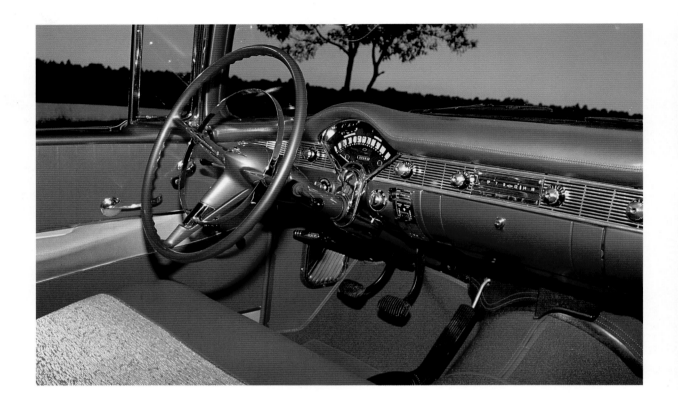

Although the instrument panel design was basically a carry over from 1955, a new option for '56 was a padded dashboard, priced at $16.15. This particular '56 Bel Air also includes a shoulder harness, another optional safety feature introduced that year.

Right
For 1956, Chevrolet's half-bird/half-jet hood ornament motif continued in familiar fashion, but the company logo badge below differed depending on power choice. A six-cylinder-equipped '56 Chevy wore a large Bow-Tie emblem identical to those on all '55 models. Choosing an optional V-8 replaced that emblem with a smaller Bow-Tie badge accompanied beneath by a large "V."

E very driving control
is easy to reach; every
instrument is easy to read.
Riding is like riding on a cloud.
—*Everything About a 56 Chevy*

Previous pages
**The flat, twin exhaust extensions tip-off the
presence of one of Chevrolet's top performing
265ci V-8s for 1956: either the single four-barrel,
205hp engine or the dual four-barrel Corvette
rendition. In this case, it's the 225hp Corvette
V-8, a $242.10 option. Also notice the optional,
rear-mounted antenna. Base price for a '56 Bel
Air sport coupe was $2,275.**

**The driver of a '56 Chevy still couldn't see this
clock, but the layout remained attractive
nonetheless. Notice the optional padded dash
and the absence of the countless small Bow-Ties
used in 1955's dashboard appliqué.**

Described by *Mechanix Illustrated*'s veteran scribe Tom McCahill in 1956 as perhaps "the greatest competition engine ever built," the 225hp 265ci Corvette V-8 introduced sports car performance to passenger car customers. Hiding beneath that huge, black breather are two four-barrel carburetors. At Daytona Beach's speed trials in early 1956, a 225hp '56 Chevy reached 136mph. This Corvette-powered '56 Bel Air was one of the first, if not the first one built, having been specially ordered by a former GM employee months before the option was officially announced in January 1956.

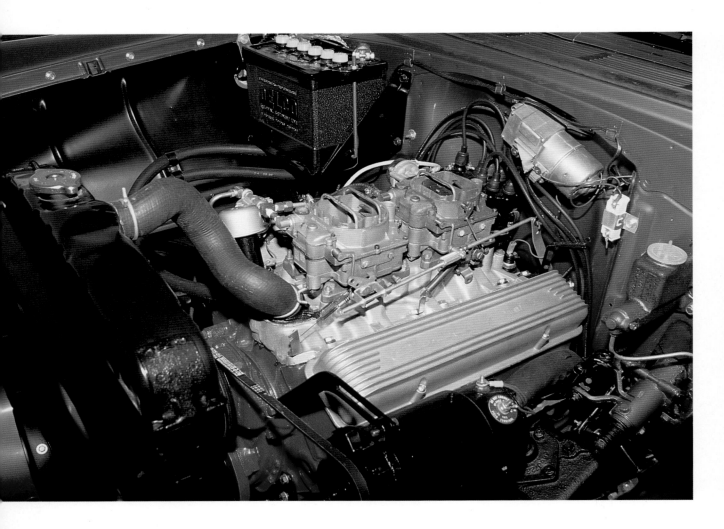

Removing the big breather exposes two four-barrel carbs each flowing about 375cfm. Included in the 225hp mix was a solid-lifter cam, 9.25:1 compression, and larger intake and exhaust ports. Originally, Chevrolet engineers wouldn't mate the dual-quad Corvette V-8 to a Powerglide, fearing the automatic wasn't up to the task. Accordingly, this early 225hp Bel Air is equipped with a three-speed manual transmission.

Right
The stylish ribbed roof and sloping pillars, a Nomad feature from beginning to end, carried over unchanged from 1955.

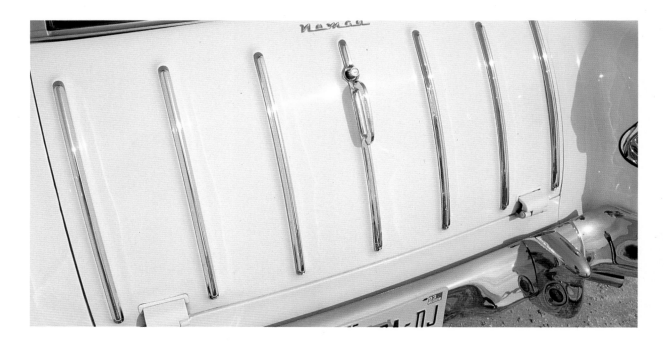

Previous pages
Chevrolet's sporty, two-door Nomad wagon returned for 1956, but sales were again disappointing, falling short of the 10,000 projected total to top out at 8,103. Nonetheless, for the second consecutive year *Motor Trend* considered the '56 Nomad to be one of the year's most beautiful automobiles. To cut costs, various exclusive features, such as the fully cut-out rear wheel openings, did not carry over from 1955. Exterior trim was pure Bel Air, save for reversing the diagonal trim slash (to match the B-pillar's forward slope) used to separate the two-tone paint just behind the door. Two-tone finishes were new for the Nomad in 1956; the '55 Nomad's exclusive trim ruled out two-toning.

Complementing the ribbed roof, these tailgate trim strips, known as "bananas," would also remain a distinctive Nomad feature. They even appeared on the '58 four-door Nomad "imposter" after the original two-door sport model had been discontinued.

Right
Folding down the Nomad's rear seat opened up loads of cargo room, more than most people realized. Nonetheless, detractors, throwing stones from a purely utilitarian perspective, simply couldn't excuse the lack of two additional doors for rearward access.

Echoing the ribbed roof design, the '56 Nomad's interior featured chrome head-liner bows.

Another 1956 cost-cutting measure did away with the '55 Nomad's exclusive "waffle pattern" interior. All '56 Nomads included basic Bel Air interior appointments.

Chapter 3

1957

Cream Of The Crop

By 1957, all of Chevrolet's lower-priced rivals had gotten their acts together, making for one of the most intensely competitive model years Detroit had ever seen. Plymouth, a company that had also rolled out a new, modern, overhead-valve V-8 in 1955, introduced a somewhat startling long, low, and wide look for '57. Likewise, arch-rival Ford debuted a totally new model that year leaving Chevrolet to take one last shot at the young, excitable market with basically the same body shell that had won everyone over in 1955.

Chevrolet made good on that shot, revamping the third rendition of the classic Chevy theme into one of the most memorable automotive creations of all time. Of course, at the time it was simply a matter of keeping pace with the competition—no one waited at the end of the production line to bestow immortal status upon these cars. Ford was charging hard that year and would, in fact, steal away the industry lead for total 1957 model year production. Creating a classic wasn't the goal at Chevrolet, staying on top was. It just so happened the two ended up running hand-in-hand.

Opposite page
While low-priced rivals from Ford and Plymouth grew lower and sleeker in 1957, Chevrolet remained with the same "high-sided" body shell introduced in 1955. However, major revamps at both ends created a look that has since epitomized fifties styling. The '57 Chevy's rear fins were restrained compared to most competing designs and nicely accentuated by ribbed, aluminum, trim inserts on each rear quarter—items exclusive to top-line Bel Airs. Lower-priced 210 models used the outline trim without the panels, while base line 150s featured a single side-spear similar to those used in 1955. Production of '57 Bel Air convertibles, priced at $2,611, was 47,562.

Ramjet fuel injection found its way into 1,530 '57 Chevys, from 150s to Bel Airs, in body styles from sedan delivery to convertible. Production of fuel injected Bel Air drop-tops was a mere sixty-eight. The most popular location for the fuel injection option was beneath the hoods of '57 Bel Air sport coupes; 524 were built.

Even with the popular, all-new Ford on the scene to share the limelight, Chevrolet wouldn't be denied, although many were quick to suggest the company was losing ground. "Never before has [Chevy] had so much to offer," claimed *Motor Life*. "And—as a matter of fact—never has it needed it more." Maintaining the same basic body while the competition updated theirs was a dangerous game, and Ford admen couldn't resist taking pot shots at Chevrolet's relatively simple face-lift. Sure, classic status would come later, but in 1957 the new Chevrolet was very nearly lost in a crowd of updated, eye-catching offerings.

Fortunately, beauty often goes beyond skin deep. Although Chevrolet's freshened '57 was by no means unattractive, the car's relative success came more in response to the package as a whole. Today, nostalgic revisionism tends to credit the '57 Chevy as a classic on looks alone. However, the car's initial popularity was based on engineering with an emphasis on performance. Chevrolet had ignited the "Hot One" legacy in 1955; two years later, rivals still couldn't touch it.

More power was one of Chevrolet's main selling points in 1957. Engineers bored out the 265ci V-8 to 283ci that year, then topped it with optional Ramjet fuel injection to help produce one horsepower per cubic inch. Even though promotional people erred by claiming Chevrolet was the first to reach this mark (Chrysler did it the year before), the achievement was impressive nonetheless.

The golden look was new for 1957 Bel Airs and was supplied by various trim pieces front and rear. Along with the V-8 emblems and Chevrolet script on the hood and trunk, Bel Air grilles, front fender hash marks, and rear quarter script all received the gold treatment in an effort to enhance the top-line image.

Equally impressive was Chevrolet's entire V-8 lineup, which featured four optional engines each with more horsepower than 1956's top offering.

In the end, Ford won 1957's model year war while Chevrolet managed to claim honors for calendar year production—by a scant 130 cars—thanks primarily to sales of its all-new '58 model. Some thirty-five years later, everyone remembers the '57 Chevy, and rightly so. As for the '57 Ford, followers shouldn't be at all ashamed of finding themselves overshadowed by a true classic.

"Looking back, I think it was our [styling staff's] objective to make a Chevrolet look like a 'little Cadillac.' Why *not* give people who could afford a Chevrolet that Cadillac look of quality."
—Carl Renner, from *The Hot Ones*, Chevrolet: 1955-1957

Inside, the '57 Chevrolet received a new steering wheel and totally redesigned "Command Post" dashboard featuring a three-pod instrument cluster. The symmetrical, twin-cowl look used in 1955 and '56 was gone, but the full-width dash face appliqué remained. The optional traffic light viewer remained as well.

T he '57 Chevy goes 'em all one better—with exciting new looks . . . zippy new power . . . luxurious new interiors . . .
—1957 advertisement

Above
Adding a center spinner helped update the familiar look of the '57 Bel Air's wheel cover. Chevrolet switched from 15in wheels to 14in for '57 models.

With the '55-56 twin-cowl motif gone, the '57 Bel Air's dashboard script and clock were arranged side by side within the bright appliqué. At last, the clock was somewhat visible to the driver.

The venerable 265ci small-block remained the standard V-8 for manual transmission applications in 1957, but was joined on the options list by six 283ci V-8s. Both the Powerglide and the new Turboglide automatic were mated to the 185hp 283ci V-8, which featured a two-barrel carburetor. If more power was desired, there was a 220hp 283ci with a single four-barrel, a 245hp 283ci with dual four-barrels, and a 250hp 283ci with Ramjet fuel injection, all available with manual or automatic transmissions. State-of-the-art passenger car performance could be had only by ordering the close-ratio three-speed manual paired with either the twin-carb 270hp 283ci or the fuel injected 283hp 283ci. The V-8 shown is the 220hp 283ci featuring 9.5:1 compression.

Previous pages
While other automakers turned towards cleaner, less cluttered sheet metal, Chevrolet dressed up its revised '57 model with various trim tricks, including twin wind-splits on the hood and eye-catching aluminum rear quarter inserts (for Bel Airs). A slightly lowered hood line for the '57 Chevrolet resulted in more windshield glass area.

According to stylist Carl Renner, accentuating the '57 Chevrolet's large, gleaming, grille/bumper design and adding rear fins was part of an attempt to associate the low-price Chevy with GM's top-line Cadillacs. Originally stylists had hoped to exit exhausts through the simulated openings below the taillights, but problems with exhaust gas staining on Cadillac bumpers using that design ruled out the plan. This Dusk Pearl hardtop is one of 166,426 Bel Air sport coupes built for 1957.

The Bel Air's various gold-plated trim pieces were also part of the styling crew's strategy to give the '57 Chevrolet a touch of Cadillac appeal. The license plate frame, yet another optional trim item, was available in either chrome or gold.

Left
As in '55 and '56, the '57 Chevrolet options list included a wide array of trim baubles, such as this door handle shield. Guards for the bumpers, grille, and door edges brightened the picture, as did lower body sill moldings.

75

Chevrolet's optional power brakes were offered in two forms dependent upon transmission choice. Standard transmission '57 Chevys were equipped with a self-contained power brake system with a built-in vacuum reservoir. Automatic transmission cars used a design featuring a separate vacuum reserve tank (silver unit to the right of the master cylinder). Price for power brakes was $37.70.

Right
Chevrolet's 210 line was usually priced about $120 lower than comparable models in the more prestigious Bel Air series and cut costs by using less pizzazz. Below the 210s, the bottom-line 150s slashed prices even further and were, at best, austere reflections of the classic Chevy image. With a production run of 162,090, the 210 two-door sedan was Chevrolet's fourth most popular model in 1957. The four-door 210 topped the list at 260,401.

Left
The standard wheel cover on 210s and 150s was this "dog dish" hubcap, an item in keeping with the budget-conscious appeal of Chevrolet's two lesser model lines. While 150s were basically cheap transportation, 210s could be dressed up considerably with optional trim and appearance pieces.

Previous pages
The most noticeable difference between a Bel Air and a 210 in 1957 was the missing aluminum trim insert on each rear quarter panel and a "Chevrolet" script in place of the appropriate "Bel Air" badge. All powertrain options available to Bel Air customers were also offered to 210 buyers. This 210 sedan is powered by a rare 270hp 283ci with dual four-barrel carburetors.

Chevrolet's middle-of-the-road 210 series lacked the Bel Air's golden trim treatment; its grille and various emblems were chrome. The 210 and 150 lines also lacked the three hash marks found on Bel Air front fenders.

It's sweet, smooth and sassy
with new velvety V-8
power, new roadability, a new
ride and everything it takes to
make you the relaxed master of
any road you travel.
—*1957 advertisement*

In keeping with the 210 model line's basic intentions, this '57 sedan came without a radio or clock—notice the two plates covering the respective openings on the dashboard's face.

Right
Chevrolet offered two versions of its dual-quad 283ci V-8 in 1957: a 245hp version and the truly hot 270hp rendition featuring a special performance solid-lifter cam. Compression was 9.5:1 for both twin-carb V-8s. While the 245hp 283ci could be paired with any transmission, the 270hp small-block was only mated to a close-ratio three-speed manual. A large, triangular air cleaner sat atop these two four-barrel carburetors and completely obscured the engine below.

T hese hot engines will enable Chevy owners to jump out into the left lane, pass and hop back into the right lane in less time than ever before and will also require . . . quicker reactions and better judgement than ever before.
—*Car Life*, February 1957

This crossed-flag script was all a stoplight challenger needed to see in 1957. On the fender's other side lurked either of two available Ramjet fuel injected 283ci V-8s, one rated at 250hp, the other at 283hp.

Previous pages
A Bel Air convertible represented the top of the Chevrolet line in 1957. When armed with a 283hp fuel injected V-8, a '57 Bel Air convertible also stood at the head of Detroit's passenger car performance pack. Listed under option number 578, Ramjet fuel injection was priced at $550 in 1957. The option was identified by crossed-flag emblems on both front fenders.

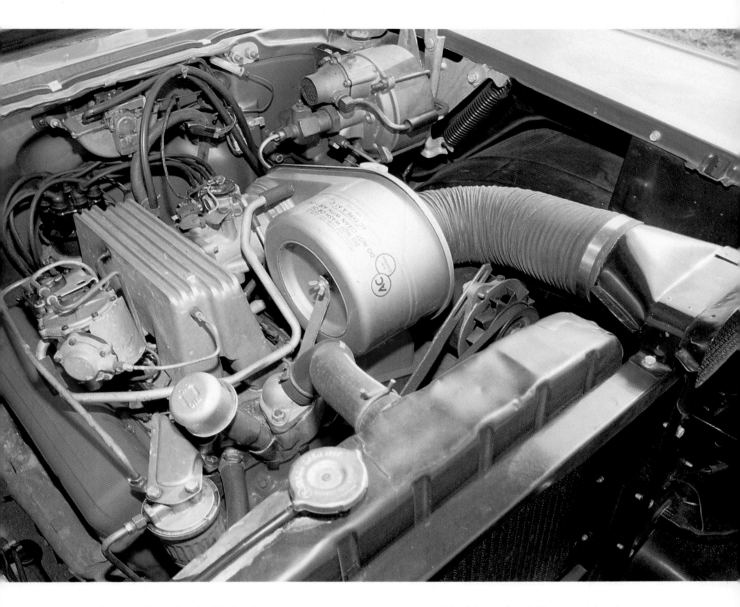

The GM designed Ramjet fuel injection system incorporated a two-piece aluminum manifold and was supplied by Rochester. To the right of the ribbed, aluminum intake plenum is the air meter assembly with its large air cleaner and induction hose; to the left is the fuel metering unit. Injector nozzles directly above the intake ports sprayed fuel into the airflow running from the manifold to the cylinder head. Chevrolet's fuel injected V-8s used solid-lifter cams and two different compression ratios: 9.5:1 for the 250hp "fuelie," 10.5:1 for the 283hp maximum performance variety.

Chevrolet's sporty Nomad two-door wagon made its final appearance in 1957, still wearing the attractive, forward-sloping roof treatment that had first appeared at the 1954 Motorama.

Production was 6,534. At $2,857, the 1957 Nomad was once again Chevy's most expensive model.

Nomad sport wagons featured sliding-glass side windows.

Following pages
Like the '56 Nomad, the '57 model was basically a Bel Air from the roof posts down, save for the unique sloping tailgate. The ribbed roof and seven tailgate "bananas" remained distinctive, exclusive features.

Nomads featured a fold-down rear seat that dropped with relative ease to open up a reasonably spacious cargo area. Volume was 36cu-ft with the seat up; 71cu-ft with it down.

Destined to grace future, mundane station wagons, this golden Nomad emblem made its last appearance on the tailgate of a truly sporty two-door wagon in 1957.

Left
The 1955 Nomad wagon had included an exclusive interior with waffle-pattern vinyl. In 1956 and '57, the Nomad interior featured typical Bel Air appointments. This '57 Nomad is equipped with optional power windows.

Right
Power options were a big deal in the fifties, and GM was no stranger to advertising their presence. Chevrolets equipped with vacuum-assisted power brakes received this advertisement on the brake pedal.

Index